Embroidered Landscapes

Kit Pyman

Search Press

Hill view, by Marion Brookes
Design based on a sketch, transferred freehand to calico with a poker pen. Machine and hand embroidery in stranded cottons. 4 × 5½in (10 × 14cm).

Introduction

Landscapes offer a great variety of subjects for embroiderers, with opportunities to explore colour, texture, mood, light and shade in all kinds of locations. The illustrations in this book range from a mountain panorama to the corner of an orchard. Many are based upon photographs. There is no need to be good at drawing to work an embroidered landscape, as a combination of photography, observation and practical experiments can result in a satisfying personal interpretation of the subject.

Now that reliable fabric paints are easily available, backgrounds can be coloured as well as stitched, and a good effect can be achieved with less time and effort than in the past.

This book aims to help you to translate a picture of a landscape into an embroidery; to choose a viewpoint, make a working drawing, transfer the design, colour the fabric with paint if you wish, decide on suitable techniques and stretch and mount the finished work.

The techniques described include hand and machine-embroidery, painting, transfer printing and spraying, appliqué, quilting and wrapping.

Ideas

Ideas may come from many sources, such as holiday snapshots and sketches, postcards, illustrations, memory, or a vision in the mind's eye.

Some embroiderers are inspired by a particular fabric, or by the desire to try out an interesting technique.

Uses

Depending on the size and technique, embroidered landscapes can be used as cushions, book covers, greetings cards, box tops and even quilts. However, for reasons of simplicity, all the ones shown in this book are intended as panels (pictures), designed to be framed and hung on the wall.

Although embroiderers are modest about their achievements, their work is often more valuable than they realise. A well framed panel sealed behind glass and kept in a dry and shaded atmosphere will last about a hundred years. It will gain in historical interest and family remembrance as time goes by, especially if it is signed and dated.

Subject

Choose a subject which rouses your enthusiasm, and which will be a rewarding investment of your time and energy. If you have a camera or can sketch, take several pictures of your chosen landscape from different angles.

Take close-up views as well, noting such details as the type of terrain, (clay soil, pebbles, etc), the shape and textures of plants, and the distribution of light and shade.

Notes, sketches and samples will all come in useful for the design.

tracing of u holiday snapshot

using card frames to choose an area

Design

The design will be based upon your own view of the subject, and arrangement of the elements you wish to include in your picture to make an attractive composition.

Begin by spreading out your material, such as pictures, photos, notes and colour references and think which features you would most like to include in the final picture.

Choice of area

You can use the whole of your photo or drawing or you can select an area and enlarge it. It is a great help to have a couple of L-shaped cards to use as a frame, as shown in the diagram. You can move the pieces about on your picture until you are satisfied with the framed view.

Foreground

You can arrange your design so that interesting features are brought into focus, and if you find a texture that is particularly attractive, you can give yourself the opportunity for some detailed stitchery.

In the tracing of the snapshot shown here, the stone wall and the leaves above had interesting textures, so these have been brought into the foreground.

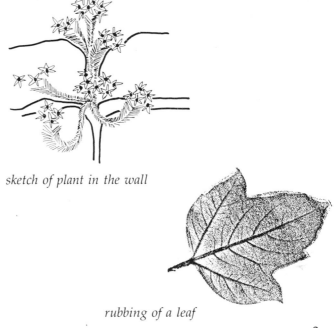

sketch of plant in the wall

rubbing of a leaf

Seascape, by Rey Crimmen
*The design was derived from her watercolour of the same scene, and transferred
freehand to calico. Coloured in fabric paints. The breakwater is applied scrim, and
net is used to represent reflections. Embroidered with a variety of stitches and
threads, and objects to hand such as plastic net, metal ring and chain.*
15½ × 11in (39 × 28cm).

View of Tenerife, by Dilys Manoy
The design was based on sketches of a swimming pool in Tenerife. Enlarged
freehand and airbrushed on to white felt cotton, using stencil shapes and potato
printing. Appliqué with silk organza, and machine embroidery, with dyed threads
and fabrics.
18 × 15in (46 × 38cm).

Viewpoint

Subjects can be seen from many angles, from far or near, above or below; they can be framed within an arch, seen through a window, or viewed from under the boughs of a tree.

framing a view

Different views can be presented on the same panel, by arranging parts of a scene within the overall view. These insets are often framed within silk wrapped borders, (see page 30).

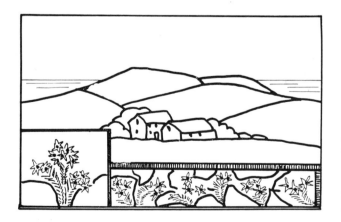

Light and shade

Study your original source of design to determine the direction of the light, as the whole mood of the landscape is affected by the way the light falls.

The distribution of light and shade can indicate both the time of year and the time of day. The sky is relatively bright in relation to the earth in spring, and darkens in winter.

Distance can be suggested by variations in tone; generally the foreground is bright and clear, the middle ground lighter and less detailed, and the far distance pale and faint in outline.

Choice of technique

Panels can combine several different techniques. The background may be painted, the fields machine-embroidered and the foreground stitched by hand. In order to decide which methods would suit your own design and particular talents, make some small experiments with fabric, paint and stitchery.

Experiments

If the background is to be painted, try out a few different colouring techniques on your chosen background fabric. Make a collection of interesting fabrics. You may find a print which perfectly represents a particular texture. Alternatively, with experiment you can build up your own texture with scraps of material and stitchery.

A soft, rolling landscape may suggest quilting, or the trunks of trees could be wrapped with textured wools. Try out quilting and wrapping on a small scale.

Practical experimentation can become quite addictive; it will give you firm ideas about your abilities and preferences, and will help to resolve any problems you may have in making a choice between techniques.

Size

The illustrations in this book look uniform in size because of the format, but in reality they range from a postcard to a large panel.

You might think that the bigger the piece the longer it will take to work but, in embroidery, the technique matters more than the size. A small piece of hand embroidery may well take longer than a large painted and applied panel.

Working drawings

By now your design will probably be a combination of tracing, sketching, notes and scribbles, within the chosen area of the original picture, but you will know what you wish to include and will have a general idea of the methods you are going to use.

Make a clean tracing of the design, and enlarge or reduce it to the exact required size. This will become your working drawing.

It is a good idea to make several photocopies of this drawing. One can be used for colour notes and another to try out tonal gradations. Extra copies can be cut up as templates for appliqué, or used for masking areas if the fabric is to be sprayed with colour.

Enlarging and reducing designs

Designs can be scaled up and down by various methods, as follows:
1. A photographic negative, or a selected area of it, can be sent for processing and the print enlarged or reduced, as required.
2. A photograph, sketch or tracing can be enlarged or reduced on a photocopier.

3. A transparency can be projected on to a sheet of paper and drawn out.

You can alter designs yourself by making a tracing, squaring it up and re-drawing it on a larger or smaller grid, as follows:
a. Trace off the design, and enclose the area in a square or rectangle.
b. Divide it into equal squares. The more complicated the design, the greater the number of divisions. Number the squares as shown.

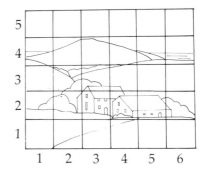

c. Take a piece of paper the required size, and divide it into the same number of equal sized squares, (this can be done by folding as well as by pencil and ruler). Number them in the same way.
d. Copy the design freehand, square by square.

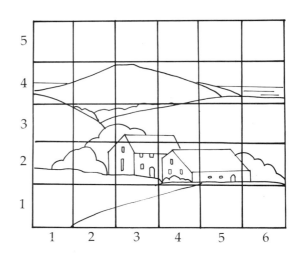

Hills and poppies, by Gladys Burley
Sketched directly on to the fabric with gouache. The net was applied to the hills while the paint was still wet. The foreground is embroidered with French knots, split and stem stitch and added felt circles.
7½ × 4½in (19 × 11cm).

Electricity my way, by Jan McGrory
The design was based upon a photograph of the local power station, and transferred by a combination of tacking and chalk. The polycotton background was spray-dyed in greys and greens, and the piece worked entirely in stem stitch in a variety of threads.
8½ × 7½in (21 × 19cm)

Sea view, by Myrna Watts
Designed from a personal sketch and transferred by water-soluble pen. Background fabrics of calico and furnishing fabric coloured with fabric paints. Embroidered with free machine embroidery over bonded and frayed-edge fabrics.
6in (15cm) square.

Country path, by Marion Brookes
Designed from a photograph and sketches, transferred freehand on to calico with a poker pen and then coloured with fabric paint. Quilted, and embroidered in stranded cotton. 4in (10cm) square.

Choice of fabric

A firm, plain, pale-coloured fabric, such as medium-weight calico, makes a good general background for a first project. Furnishing fabric and some dress fabrics are suitable, but avoid loose and stretchy weaves.

If you intend to colour the fabric, check that the fibre content is compatible with the type of paint you wish to use.

For some types of colouring, fabric needs to be washed before use, so check on this before transferring the design.

Allow enough material for a good margin round the work. An extra piece is useful for stitch and paint experiments.

Preparation of fabric

Cut it out by the thread. If it is likely to fray, oversew, zig-zag or tape over the raw edges. Iron it if necessary. Mark central vertical and horizontal lines with running stitches. This helps to align the design on the fabric, and centre the fabric on the frame.

Transferring the design

In general the design is transferred to the fabric before it is coloured or framed up, but this is not always so. If you are going to colour the fabric, check on the technique you intend to use before you start. A transfer print, for example, can be drawn on paper and ironed on to the fabric, and some kinds of background spraying and painting need only the simplest of paper templates.

The most detailed method of transferring a design is to trace it through a dressmakers' carbon, or to make a transfer print as shown on page 15.

If your design is likely to change during its progress, choose a method which is not permanent, such as the sewing or the template method, or use a washable embroidery pencil.

Tracing method

Trace off your design on to tracing paper, marking central vertical and horizontal lines. Tape or pin the prepared fabric to a flat surface. Lay a piece of dressmakers' carbon face down over the fabric. Lay the tracing over the carbon,

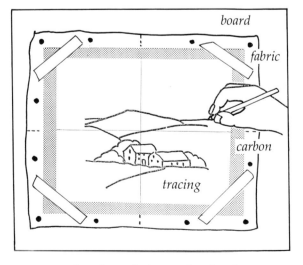

tracing through dressmakers' carbon

face upwards, and align the vertical and horizontal lines. Make sure all three layers are secured to the board.

Using a sharp hard pencil, trace round the design with firm pressure. Turn up a corner and check that all the lines are transferred before taking off the carbon.

Sewing method

Trace the design on to tissue paper. Position this on the fabric, right side up, and secure with pins. Sew along all the lines through both layers with small running stitches. Score the tissue along the lines to split the paper, then pull gently away.

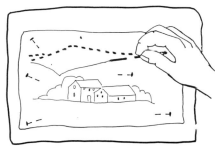

sewing through tissue paper

Template method

Trace the design on to tracing paper, then glue it on to stiff paper or thin card. Cut out the shapes. Lay them in position on the fabric and mark round them with running stitches, chalk or washable embroidery pencil.

If the design is to be quilted, templates are laid on the fabric and scratched round with a needle.

Templates are also used to mask out areas when the fabric is being sprayed.

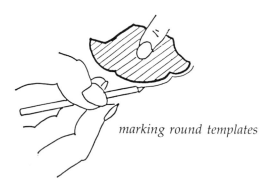

marking round templates

See-through method

Strengthen the lines of the design with black ink and tape it to a window, or on to a sheet of glass over a source of light. Lay the fabric on the glass, tape it in position, and trace the design with a washable embroidery pencil.

Frames

Frames stretch the fabric taut and allow you to see the whole picture before you as you work. If you don't already possess a frame, a home-made one will do, and has the advantage that the work can be left on. Slate and ring frames can be bought with a stand, which leaves both hands free. Ring frames are only suitable for small pieces of work.

Ring frame or embroidery hoop

A ring frame consists of one wooden ring fitted inside another, between which the fabric is tensioned.

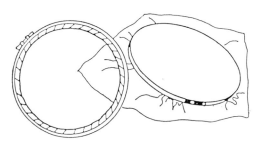

two sections of ring frame

Lay the fabric, right side up, over the inner ring. Press the outer ring over it, and pull the fabric out gently until it is taut. Try to keep the grain straight. Tighten the screw with a screwdriver. If the fabric slips, bind the inner ring with strips of cotton.

11

12

Winter walk on the Ridgeway, by Marie Whitworth
The design was taken from a photograph, and transferred by the sewing method. Background of painted calico, embroidered with straight stitch, split stitch, French knots and tufting.
4 × 6in (10 × 15cm).

Winter through the window, by Ann Richards
Designed from a photograph, and transferred by painting and the sewing method. Appliqué in organza and net, some quilting and free surface stitchery in stranded cottons and metallic thread.
7½ × 5½in (19 × 14).

Winter view, by Vera Bradshaw
Designed from photographs and sketches, and transferred by the sewing method to a calico ground overlaid with organza. Worked in appliqué, shadow work and free stitchery. Mounted in a deep frame, representing a window.
8 × 6in (20 × 15cm).

Home-made frame

Home-made frames can be made of artists' stretchers, old wooden picture frames, or of four pieces of wood joined together, and made to the exact size required.

The fabric is attached to the frame with staples or drawing pins, (thumbtacks). Panels are often left on the frame when they are finished, thus saving stretching and mounting. If the work is to be left on, attach the fabric at the back; if the frame is temporary, attach the fabric on the front.

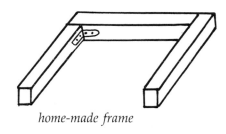

home-made frame

fabric on front of home-made frame

fabric folded to back of home-made frame

lap frame

standing frame

Colouring fabrics

There is a wide choice available today in paints and crayons for colouring fabric.

Starter kits can be bought in artists' supply shops. Three simple methods are outlined below:
1. Direct application of paint.
2. Transfer printing.
3. Spraying.

First read the instructions and see what type of fabric is recommended. Some colours work on natural fibres and some on man-made, so choose your background fabric accordingly.

Direct painting and spraying are best done on a taut surface. Thin fabric should be framed, to keep it clear of a wet background which will make the colours run. Thicker fabrics should be stretched on a board over a few layers of newsprint covered with a clean sheet of paper, secured all round with drawing pins, (thumbtacks), staples or tape.

Direct paint

You will need a few pots of water-soluble paints in primary colours, a large and a small brush and some plastic pots for mixing colours.

Work on flat stretched fabric. Washes of thin colour can be applied to wet fabric with a large brush. When this is dry, details can be put in with a fine brush. Drying can be speeded up by using a hair dryer.

Textured effects can be achieved with a thicker mixture of paint, dabbed on with a sponge or piece of crumpled tissue. More defined shapes can be made by printing with corks or cut potatoes, or dabbing through roughly cut stencils.

Don't forget to fix the colour by applying heat, according to the paint manufacturer's instructions.

Transfer prints

A quick and simple way to transfer a design on to fabric is by making your own colour transfer.

A small packet of crayons will be enough, as the picture will not be detailed. Make sure they are designed for 'transfer printing' and not for crayoning straight on to the fabric.

Colours change when they are transferred, so rub samples on to a piece of paper and iron this off on to a spare piece of the background fabric as a reference. The more synthetic fibres there are in your fabric, the stronger the colours will be.

As transfers reverse the image, trace off, or photocopy your working drawing on to tracing paper, and colour it in on the back. Iron off according to the manufacturer's instructions.

Textures can be directly transferred. As an example, rub crayon over a leaf, lay it on the fabric, cover with a cloth and transfer the rubbing with a hot iron.

transfer print made with crayons

Spraying

This is a quick way of applying general background colours; the drawback is that the paint spreads around as you spray and you need to cover up a large area of floor and wall. Some people work in the garage or in the garden.

A basic starter set will consist of a few little mixer bottles and a can of compressed air.

A water-based fabric paint is used, which can be diluted. Wash and iron the fabric and stretch it on a board. Prop this up against the wall, having already protected the surface. Start spraying beyond the board and then sweep lightly across. Several fine layers are better than one thick one, which might drip.

Spraying can produce a faint all-over tint, or reproduce the shading of an evening sky. It can be used to depict shadows or highlights.

A swift way of applying a design straight on to the fabric is to spray in the main areas in different colours. Make a tracing of the whole design and cut it up into sections, for example, sky, lake, middle distance and foreground. Using these sections as masks, spray each area in turn with the chosen colour.

Poker work

This is hardly colouring, but it is another method of marking fabric. Poker pens can now be bought in craft shops, and the heat produces a variety of effects from a delicate sepia line to a deep scorch.

Threads

Colour your threads at the same time as you are colouring the fabrics by soaking them in whichever solution you are using. Don't forget to apply heat when they are dry to fix the colour.

A collection of threads containing various fibres will take up the colour in different ways, and will provide an interesting range of shades to tone with the fabric.

If you would like the colours to be shaded or have a random effect, wind the threads on to cards and dab one side only with fabric paint.

English landscape
by Hiroko Higashi
The design was adapted from a
picture in a book. Painted and
embroidered on one fabric, it was
cut out and quilted to a calico
background.
13 × 9½in (33 × 24cm).

Machine embroidery

The sewing machine is a useful tool and can be used for appliqué, quilting, texturing and making decorative lines. Any modern machine fitted with a motor and swing needle will work machine embroidery.

Machine embroidery using the presser-foot

With the machine set up for ordinary sewing, decorative effects can be made with both stitches and threads. Fabric should be firm and non-stretchy. It can be manipulated in the hands, or mounted in a frame, (see opposite page).

Threads

Ordinary sewing threads can be used as for dressmaking, and effects achieved by variation of stitch and colour.

Buttonhole twist can be used as the top thread, as well as some embroidery silks.

Textured threads can be couched in place with a line of zig-zag.

Thick, or metallic threads, can be wound on to the bobbin spool by hand. If you do this, the bottom tension will have to be slackened according to the instructions for your machine, (many embroiderers keep a spare bobbin case just for embroidery). The spool thread appears on the underside of the fabric, so designs using thick thread have to be worked from the back.

Technique

Rows of lines, either in straight stitch, zig-zag or a combination of the two, can create both texture and pattern. Lines can be straight or curved, parallel or irregular, close together or spaced, continuous or broken.

The use of the reverse feed will create a back-and-forth effect of a wide zig-zag.

Satin stitch will give a thick rounded line. A mass of lines will make a textured area.

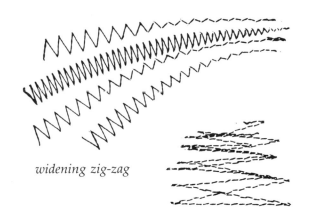
widening zig-zag

straight stitch using reverse feed

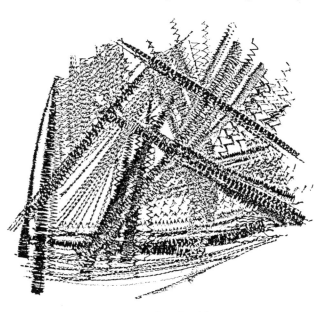
texture produced with straight stitch and zig-zag

Free machine embroidery

Free machine embroidery is often referred to as 'drawing with a needle' but, unlike drawing, the instrument stays still while the taut fabric is moved about. Prepare the machine for embroidery, or what may be referred to in the instructions as 'darning'. This usually involves lowering the feed and changing, or removing, the foot.

Fabric

Use a plain, smooth, strong fabric. Stretchy or knitted fabrics will not stay taut enough in the frame.

Framing up

Use a small ring frame with a narrow rim that will pass beneath the needle. The frame is prepared in the reverse way to hand embroidery, with the ring uppermost and the fabric in contact with the machine bed.

Place the fabric right side up over the outer ring, and press the inner ring in place. Pull the fabric very taut and tighten the screw with a screwdriver. It is essential that the surface is absolutely taut at all times for free machine embroidery.

straight stitch patterns

Hold the frame lightly at each side and move it about smoothly and evenly. Keep the fabric in close contact with the machine bed and try not to raise the ring towards the needle.

The stitch length control does not operate without the feed but the speed of the movement of the ring will control the length of stitch.

The width control operates for zig-zag. Try varying the width and moving the ring in circles, backwards and forwards, or side to side to make different outlines and textures.

Remember to keep the presser bar down at all times when you are working, otherwise the needle will not pick up the lower thread.

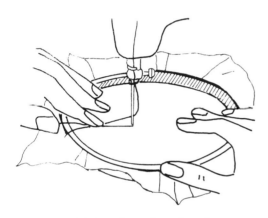

machining through a ring frame

Needle and threads

Thread the machine up with ordinary dressmaking threads to begin with, but use a stronger needle than usual.

If you are using a lot of colours, you can keep a neutral coloured thread in the bobbin and need only change the top thread.

Technique

Position the frame under the needle, *and lower the presser bar*. Take one stitch to bring up the lower thread. Holding both threads down on the fabric behind the needle, take a few more stitches to secure and then cut them off close to the fabric.

zig-zag patterns

Scottish hills and loch, by Linda Randall
The design was based on holiday memories and photographs, and transferred to the calico freehand. The sky is crayoned, and the stitches include very loose stem stitch, straight, chain and running stitches and French knots. A first attempt at an embroidered panel, to practise stitches and design.
7 × 5½in (18 × 14cm).

The river Mole near Boxhill, by Jean Robinson
The design was derived from photographs and sketches, and only the main lines were lightly transferred in pencil to the fabric, which was a rough-woven striped furnishing fabric. The 'watery' effect was achieved by withdrawing black threads and re-weaving with blue, and vice versa. The figure is in stumpwork, the background embroidered with machine appliqué and hand stitchery in various threads.   15 × 11in (38 × 28cm).

couching

French knots   cross stitch

Cross stitch

Cross stitch can be worked regularly on fabric where the threads can be counted, but it has great scope if worked irregularly on closely woven fabric, and can be adapted to all kinds of uses. You can work each cross individually, or make a more flowing line in two journeys.

The effect is smoother if you keep all the top stitches lying in the same direction.

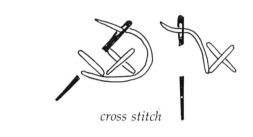

cross stitch

Hand embroidery

Although you will find hundreds of different embroidery stitches in craft books, there is hardly an outline, symbol or texture that cannot be reproduced with just a few familiar stitches. You can work them in different sizes; you can pack them together roughly or arrange them in neat rows; you can lay them down in blocks or scatter them thinly over a whole area. A change in the type of thread or the colour will alter the whole look.

Threads can be shiny or matt, thick or thin, rough or smooth.

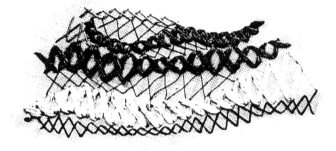

French knots

With a smooth rounded thread and one or two wraps, French knots can lie as neatly as snail shells.

If you want a bigger knot, it is better to use a thicker thread than to make too many wraps.

The diagram shows how the stitch is worked in a frame. The thumb should be kept on the loop of thread to hold the wraps tight as the needle is re-inserted into the hole.

Couching

Any thread which will not go through the fabric, (as well as cords, braids and narrow strips of fabric), can be laid on the background and couched down with a finer thread.

Groups of threads can be couched at irregular intervals, leaving loose fibres ballooning out or hanging down in loops.

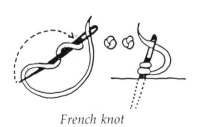

French knot

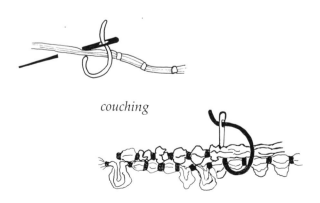

couching

Straight stitch

The simplest and most flexible embroidery stitch, consists of a single line. Tiny straight stitches in different directions are called 'seeding', or 'speckling', and are very useful for subtle shading.

Stitch direction can convey both movement and structure, as in the sketches of trees below.

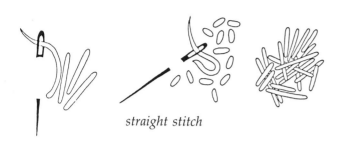

straight stitch

Cypress, pine and cherry trees in straight stitch

Chain stitch

This is a looped stitch which can be used singly, as a line, or to fill areas. The tail of a detached chain can be greatly lengthened to accentuate direction.

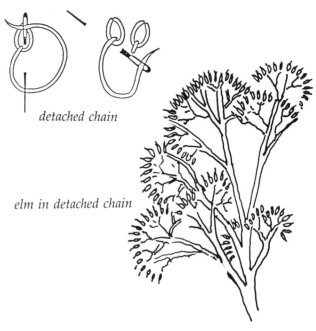

detached chain

elm in detached chain

Fly stitch

This is another stitch which can be used singly, arranged in patterns or made into a line. The 'tail' can be lengthened, and the length of the arms can also be varied.

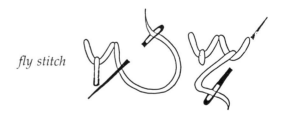

fly stitch

fly stitch

detached chain

detached fly stitch

straight stitch

Sunset, by Marjorie Lawrence
The design was adapted from a calender, and transferred freehand to the fabric.
Worked in surface stitchery and appliqué on a furnishing fabric in a variety of silks
and cottons.
7 × 5in (18 × 13cm).

Landscape, by Pauline Bannon
A design suggested entirely by fabrics, which are laid in layers, using plain cottons,
striped furnishing fabric, plastic coated fabric, and curtain net over all.
Embroidered in quilting, straight stitching and French knots.
8 × 6in (20 × 15cm).

Appliqué

This is the technique of applying one fabric to another, using hand or machine stitchery or adhesives.

For decorative use, there is no need to make a neat edge, indeed, a frayed edge is often an advantage. Also, there is no need to match the grain with that of the background, except for large pieces which might pucker.

Fabric

Use a strong background fabric. All types of material can be used for appliqué—woven or non-woven.

Layers of organza can give depth and colour to a sky; knobbly tweed may imitate the texture of bark, and scraps of painted interlining, or scorched leather, may represent a stone wall.

Texture, colour and reflective qualities are all important. A shiny fabric will stand out, a matt one will recede. A thick pile looks darker in tone than a smooth one. Shot silks can be arranged to catch the light. Transparent fabrics can be used over stitchery or paint to suggest translucency.

Fabric can be altered before being applied by painting, scorching, folding, fraying or texturing with stitchery.

Hand appliqué

Frame up the background fabric. Make a paper template, (see page 11), of the shape to be applied, and lay it on the appliqué fabric. Pin them together, mark round the template with chalk or washable embroidery pencil and then cut out, allowing for a hem if you wish.

Position the cut-out shape on the background and secure with a pin, or tack with long slanting stitches, (not round the edge). You can secure the edge invisibly with stab stitch, accentuate it with a line stitch or couched cord, or blur it with stitchery that shades off into the background.

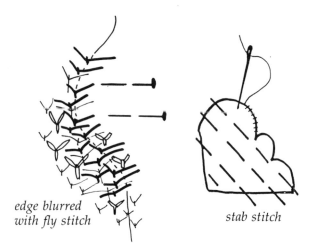

edge blurred with fly stitch

stab stitch

If you would like the shape to stand out, cut a piece of wadding fractionally smaller and apply the wadding beneath the cut-out shape to the background.

Machine appliqué

This can be done with the foot on the machine, or with free embroidery.

To stitch round the edge

Using a template as described, (page 11), mark the shape on the appliqué fabric and cut it out some distance beyond the line. Position the shape on the background fabric and pin or

appliqué with stitched edge

tack, then go round the marked lines with straight stitch. Trim away the fabric, and go over the lines again with a narrow zig-zag.

To stitch over the applied piece

Stitchery need not be limited to the outline; lines of straight stitching across the shape can look almost like quilting, and lines of open zig-zag will create contours and textures.

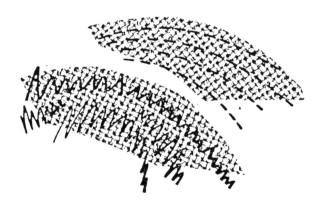

appliqué with overstitching

Appliqué with adhesives

Attach the piece with a fabric adhesive according to the manufacturer's instructions. Use sparingly, as you may need to stitch through the stiffened fabric.

Iron-on interfacing is often used in its own right; it comes in different weights, will take paint or dye, and can easily be cut into complicated shapes.

Fabrics can be closely bonded together with fusible webbing, ironed on according to the manufacturer's instructions. Check that your fabrics will stand the recommended heat of the iron.

glued scraps of painted interfacing

A free and more random type of appliqué can be used to build up interesting textures, with the use of bonding paper. Take a piece of paper larger than the chosen area, and tear off a corner, which will expose the edge of the adhesive web. Detach the web carefully, pull it into pieces and scatter it over the background fabric. On this base arrange your scraps of fabric, ravelled thread, paper etc., and when you are satisfied with the effect, lay a piece of baking parchment over it all and press with a hot iron. Hand or machine embroidery can then be added.

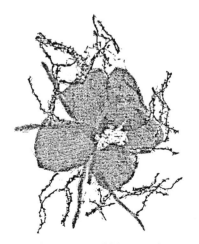

*fragments of fabric and
thread secured with adhesive web*

The river in winter, by Pamela Powell
The design was derived from a photograph, and painted on to cotton stretched on a frame with fabric paints. Bushes and tree outlines in machine embroidery. Applied lining fabric is used for the river, the banks being built up with cotton wool overlaid with non-woven fabric and satin. Stones and glass beads were applied, with some surface stitchery.
17 × 25in (43 × 62cm).

Rape field, by Marie Whitworth
An idea worked out in wrapping, using various textures of wool around card. A few added stitches indicate the fence and the tree.
7 × 5in (18 × 13cm).

Quilting

Quilting is the stitching together of several layers of fabric. In landscape panels it is a way of contouring the surface, either in areas, (wadded quilting), or in small sections, (trapunto quilting).

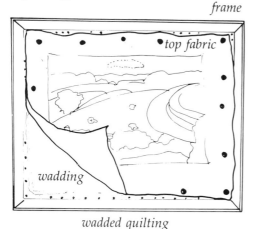

wadded quilting

Wadded quilting

Stretch a strong background fabric in a frame, cover with wadding, lay over the top fabric, (which may already be coloured and marked with the design), and pin or tack lightly in place. Stitch through all three layers with running or back stitch.

If the design is not marked, cut a card template, (page 11), lay it in place, and mark round with a sharp needle. The scratch should still be visible while the stitchery is being worked.

Trapunto quilting

Transfer the design to the top fabric, and sew this and the backing fabric firmly together. Turn over, cut a slit in the backing and stuff the shape with wool or wadding, packing it in firmly. Sew up the slit.

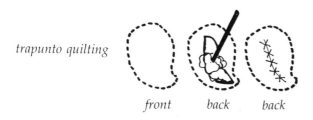

trapunto quilting

front   back   back

Wrapping

Winding threads round a piece of card or a frame is an ingenious way of producing an impression of a landscape, see page 29.

Wrapped card

Wind double-sided tape round a piece of card, and then wrap it horizontally with different colours and textures of thread. Sections of card can be wrapped vertically and stuck on. Shapes like the sun or a tree can be embroidered over the wrapped thread, or made of pieces of weaving, knitting, crochet etc.

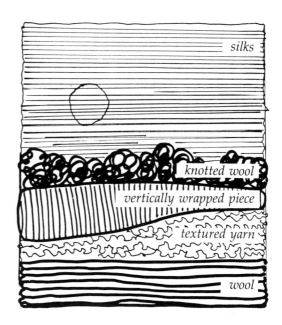

Wrapped frames

Narrow strips of card covered with silk or wool thread can be used as an inner frame to link an embroidered panel to a mount, or to divide a panel into different areas, as in the diagram on page 6.

Use 6-sheet mounting board, and cut narrow bands, or the required outline with a craft knife and a steel rule. Apply double-sided tape to the reverse and commence wrapping, peeling down the protective paper as you go.

Threads can be started and finished off with scraps of tape. At the corners, paint the card to match the wrapping.

Finishing off

Embroidery which has been taken off a frame will need to be set in shape by 'stretching' before being mounted or framed.

Stretching

The following process squares up the fabric and 'irons' it without flattening the surface:
1. Place some sheets of wet blotting paper or wrung out towelling on a board.
2. Pin lengths of string across the board, outlining the required finished size.
3. Place the embroidery within these lines, right side up. Using rustless drawing pins, (thumbtacks), pin and stretch the fabric to shape, starting at the centre of each side and working outwards. Check measurements constantly and ensure the sides are at right angles.
4. Leave to dry naturally, for however long it takes.

stretching

Mounting

Cut a piece of hardboard the required size. Mark the centre of each side. Lay it on the back of the embroidery, matching centre lines. Fold the fabric over to the back and secure by sticking pins into the cut edge working from the centre of each side to the corners. Keep looking at the front to see if the panel is straight. When you reach the corners, trim the fabric and fold it down.

The loose fabric can then be glued or laced at the back. The safest adhesives are made of polyvinyl acetate. Apply as thinly as possible and keep away from the edge.

Use a long strong thread for lacing. Start in the middle and work outwards, first horizontally and then vertically, and adjust and tighten until the fabric fits snugly. Cover the back with plain cotton fabric.

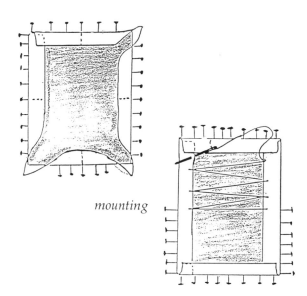

mounting

Framing

If you would like your panel to last a long time, use acid-free materials and make sure it is well insulated against dust. Seal over the stitching at the back of the mount with masking tape, seal the glass into the frame, and seal all round the back of the frame before covering with the usual gummed paper. The enemies of textiles are dust, damp and light, so hang the panel in a dry and shady place.

First published in Great Britain 1989
Search Press Ltd.
Wellwood, North Farm Road,
Tunbridge Wells, Kent TN2 3DR

Text and diagrams by Kit Pyman

Photographs by Search Press Studios

ISBN 0 85532 635 2

Dry stone wall, by Marion Brookes
*Design sketched freehand on to the background fabric.
The wall is made up of scraps of re-cycled paper.
Embroidered in cottons.
4½ × 6in (11 × 15cm).*

Typeset by Scribe Design, 123 Watling Street, Gillingham, Kent
Made and printed in Spain by A.G. Elkar S. Coop. Bilbao-12